# Connetix magnetic building tiles are an open-ended toy that grows with each child.

Connetix tiles encourage cognitive development, spatial awareness, hand-eye coordination, fine and gross motor skills and help children build knowledge around scientific and mathematical concepts, **all through play.**

 **UNIQUE BEVEL DESIGN**

 **FOOD GRADE NON-TOXIC**

 **STRONGER MAGNETS**

 **RIVETED FOR EXTRA SAFETY**

 WHERE **PLAY AND LEARNING** CONNECT

# Little Islanders

Inspired by Heritage | Crafted with Love

little-islanders.com

Born in 1949. Thousands of new configurations
yet to be discovered.

String Shelving System configured by interior
designer Lotta Agaton. Discovered in 2021.

string®

EDITOR IN CHIEF
Harriet Fitch Little

EDITOR
John Burns

ART DIRECTOR
Staffan Sundström

DESIGN DIRECTOR
Alex Hunting

ILLUSTRATOR
Espen Friberg

ADVERTISING,
SALES & DISTRIBUTION
DIRECTOR
Edward Mannering

ADVERTISING MANAGER
Jessica Gray

STUDIO & PROJECT MANAGER
Susanne Buch Petersen

DIGITAL MANAGER
Cecilie Jegsen

PROOFREADER
Taahir Husain

PUBLICATION DESIGN
Alex Hunting Studio

COVER ILLUSTRATION
Espen Friberg

WORDS
Ann Babe
Shanicia Boswell
Chie Davis
Nell Frizzell
Elle Hunt
Robert Ito
Robyn Price Pierre
Asher Ross
Caspar Salmon
Emma Scott-Child
Tom Whyman

ART & PHOTOGRAPHY
Oumayma B. Tanfous
Rodrigo Carmuega
María del Río
Espen Friberg
Sarah Hingley
Anders Kylberg
Kourtney Kyung Smith
Staffan Sundström

STYLING, SET DESIGN,
HAIR AND MAKEUP
Paloma Alcantar
Diana Choi
Emilie Florin
Lianna Fowler
Nouri Hassan
Linn Henrichson
Erol Karadağ
Ayaka Nihei
Karla Welch

PUBLISHER
Chul-Joon Park

ISSUE 01
*Kindling* is published biannually
by Ouur ApS, Amagertorv 14,
1, 1160 Copenhagen, Denmark.
Printed by Park Communications
Ltd in London, United Kingdom.
Color reproduction by Park
Communications Ltd in London,
United Kingdom. All rights
reserved. No part of this
publication may be reproduced,
distributed or transmitted in any
form or by any means, including
photocopying or other electronic
or mechanical methods, without
prior written permission of the
editor in chief, except in the
case of brief quotations embodied
in critical reviews and certain
other noncommercial uses permitted
by copyright law.

The views expressed in *Kindling*
magazine are those of the
respective contributors and are
not necessarily shared by the
company or its staff.

CONTACT US
If you have questions or
comments, please write to us at
*info@kinfolk.com*. For advertising
and partnership inquiries, get in
touch at *kindling@kinfolk.com*

STORQ

storq.com

# MamaOwl

MamaOwl believes in a *gentle* and *beautiful* childhood. Natural clothes made for *playing* and *exploring* and toys that foster *curiosity*.

**mamaowl.net** wool | cotton | sustainable | babies | kids | adults

# ISSUE ONE

Sometimes, a word can spark an idea. That's what happened at *Kinfolk* when we discovered that a magazine about fatherhood called *Kindling* had circulated for a couple of years in the early 2010s. With the blessing of its former founders, we're bringing it back to life—this time as a magazine for all people with children in their lives.

During its nine-month gestation, *Kindling* has been guided by three principles. First, it's a magazine that thinks about raising a child as a relationship that expands horizons—a time of intellectual curiosity and discovery. Second, you won't find competing opinions on the "best" way to do things—internet forums have got that covered. Third, we've avoided photographing or interviewing families in the knowledge that one person's day-to-day can be another's unhelpful yardstick for comparison. If we had a motto, it might go something like this: *Come as you are... stay until things sound suspiciously quiet in the other room.*

Our first issue runs the gamut from serious to silly. On page 60, Ann Babe asks readers to interrogate why so many support orphanages abroad who wouldn't at home. On page 24, we launch an irreverent investigation into the gruffalo's parenting style, written by a father who has clearly taken one too many trips into that deep dark wood. The back section of the magazine, Fun Stuff, is full of activities to do with children—like all of the suggestions in *Kindling*, we've designed them to be as accessible as possible.

Thank you so much for picking up our first issue. We hope you enjoy it, and that it goes on to live many lives in your home as paper planes, posters or indeed as kindling (see page 77 for how to build a fire). If you have ideas about what you'd like to see in our winter issue, send us a message on Instagram at @kindlingmagazine.

"Come as you are...stay until things sound suspiciously quiet."

Editor in Chief
**HARRIET FITCH LITTLE**

# Introducing the parents and educators who helped us along the way.

## MEET OUR EDITORIAL BOARD

SHANICIA BOSWELL

Shanicia is an author, retreat organizer and founder of the global parenting community Black Moms Blog. She interviews Meena Harris on page 36. Aged eight, her daughter Kamryn asked her: "Why are all adults so old?"

Liz (pronouns: she/her) is a school teacher and creator of the anti-bias and anti-racism educational platform Teach and Transform. She made the exercises you'll find in the Emotions section. Once, while teaching a year group with a classroom pet, a pupil asked her how many hamsters she thought she could fit in her mouth.

LIZ KLEINROCK

DAVID MICHAEL PEREZ

David co-founded the first iteration of *Kindling*, which was published between 2012 and 2015 and focussed on stories about fatherhood. His son Amon, aged eight, recently asked him: "What do you think it is like after we die; do you think it is just like before we were born?" Turn to page 27 for tips on fielding exactly this question.

ROBYN
PRICE
PIERRE

Emma runs the creative studio Ladyland, and is the author of *Quick Crafts For Parents Who Think They Hate Craft*. She made all the games and challenges you'll find at the back of the magazine. Her children would like to know what a burger made out of ravens would taste like and, relatedly, why they feel hungry every time they see hills.

Question:

Robyn is a writer, creative director and the author of *Fathers*, an art book project about Black fatherhood. She interviews Reginald Dwayne Betts on page 30. Recently, her daughter Parker, aged five, has been interested to know if bugs get sick, and why Georgie Pig (her puppet) can't drive home.

EMMA
SCOTT-CHILD

WHAT'S THE STRANGEST QUESTION A CHILD HAS ASKED YOU? (SEE PAGE 26 FOR MORE!)

## Part 1:
# FIRST STEPS

15 — 34

Look out for
captions labeled
KIDS' CORNER to
discover pathways
through the magazine
aimed at children.

## Part 2:
# BIG READS

35 — 78

"Laughing is good,
          play is essential."

P.102 — Dacher Keltner

What would you like to see listed on this page in Issue Two? Send us ideas at @kindlingmagazine on Instagram.

Part 3:

# EMOTIONS :)

Part 4:

# FUN STUFF

KIDS' CORNER
A cuddly version of our cover star, Claude, is hiding in one of our stories. Can you find him?

all the babies.

# First Steps

15 — 34

# — Empty Nest

## Minimalism is still the hottest trend in children's bedroom decor. But who's it really for?

Words
CASPAR SALMON

Surfing through parenting blogs or Pinterest boards for ideas on how to decorate children's bedrooms, a common theme emerges: the pristine minimalism of so many rooms. The aspiration is for white spaces, untroubled by clutter or colors, and arrangements that, according to your outlook, might be called either Zen or Spartan. Gone are the cozy, den-like trappings of yesterday, when kids' rooms erred on the side of maximalist accumulation—clashing patterns, beanbags, teddies galore, and duvet covers printed with various gender-straightjacketed rockets and cartoon princesses.

The overall drive for the Pinterest parent seems to err towards a tasteful *absence*. Gallery-white walls accentuate a kind of neutral quality. Perhaps this reflects a wish not to push any strong identifiers on a child—white is gender-free, of course, and goes with everything. Emilie Fournet, a London-based interior designer, points out that a child can age into a neutral room: "It will give more flexibility in the long run as the child grows up and their interests evolve," she says. She also links the tendency to a greater desire for sustainability.

Perhaps this lack of *things* stems also from the internet era, in which physical media has the potential to be obliterated by the web. Gadgets, books, DVDs, tape recorders and many games have been swallowed up by the provision of apps and streaming services. Such items no longer need to be weaved into the fabric of the room's decor, meaning that the bedroom's outlook has been pared down significantly. Or perhaps parents are actually just projecting their own tastes onto children who might otherwise appreciate a touch more coziness in their sanctum. Indeed, there can be something disturbingly adult about many decoration trends, such as one Toronto blogger's suggestion to style kids' bookshelves based on the appeal of their covers while keeping toys stored in bins in the basement.

Maria Montessori is often cited by proponents of child-centric minimalism. This checks out, insofar as Montessori believed that creativity flourishes best in uncluttered rooms, and that beauty is of objective importance to young minds. But she also, crucially, believed that a child's environment should be designed with the child's use in mind: today, that might mean a low bed, toys in cubbies rather than on shelves, and art at eye level. Give children minimalism *without* that autonomy, and you can bet on a swathe of rebellious youngsters getting into clutter in 10 years' time.**k**

Our illustrator Espen, whose drawings you'll find throughout the magazine, welcomed his first child last year. Consequently, he can only dream of a room as clutter-free as the one he's drawn here.

"It is well known that a great many difficulties rise in raising and properly housing babies and small children in crowded cities." So wrote Emma Read, of Spokane, Washington, in 1922 when she filed her patent for a Portable Baby Cage—a cage "suspended upon the exterior of a building adjacent to an open window, wherein the baby or young child may be placed." By the end of the decade, the mesh enclosures were a common sight in cities, protruding from apartment windows high above the streets of London and New York.

The idea was simple: the child gets a bit of sunshine and air, and the parent gets a half hour's peace. Eleanor Roosevelt used a crude one, though her neighbors criticized her for the noise her child made while in it. The craze for "airing" one's children was intensified by the fear of tuberculosis, against which wisdom held that fresh air was the best precaution. The fad saturated newspaper opinion columns at the time, and had less stomach-lurching expressions—such as the construction of new open-air schools. Read's own patent centers on the virtues of fresh air, and only toward the end mentions "improved" bracing materials that would keep the oxygenated child from falling into the clangor below.

The problem of where to safely put a child in order to get something done is age-old, and our guts tell us that fresh air is good for our kids. (In Nordic countries, for example, it is still commonplace to leave children in strollers outside doorways.) The more we believe that a given distraction is healthy for our child, the more freely we can turn to our own neglected thoughts and needs. Light, air, and peace were hard to come by in the densely urbanized early 20th century, and these cages, however insane they now appear, satisfied those needs.

It was not wise, of course, to suspend babies in cages above the streets. But the suspension of reason that allowed those parents to do so—the desire to reclaim a half-hour of hands-free time around the house—is still with us, and is perhaps part of how we survive to parent another day. Every era exaggerates some dangers while ignoring others. It's reasonable to expect that some of what we now deem normal will one day be considered strange—gender reveal parties, for example, or (if I'm lucky) the YouTube channel Little Baby Bum. **k**

# A stomach-lurching space management solution.

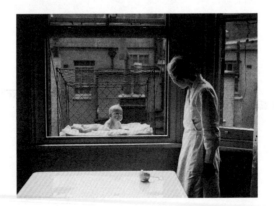

Words
ASHER ROSS

# TAMBERE

@tambere_official
www.tambere.co.kr

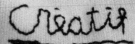

## MY BIRTHDAY CAKE

'SUBTITLE : CELEBRATION'
THERE IS NO ONE THAT DOESN'T NEED IT,
THE WHOLE WORLD NEEDS IT.

# Kids stuff that is kind to parents' eyes

# How to make (adult) friends on a play date.

## — First Words

Words
NELL FRIZZELL

Having a child can, even from the moment of conception, feel like a great portal of empathy has opened up between you and every other caregiver on the planet. I know how it feels, right down to my feet, to be that person bouncing up and down the park path, trying to shush a four-month-old to sleep in their sling. But what about when you want to talk about something other than wipes, weaning and wind?

Questions like "What do you do?" can be problematic when people are on parental leave or have perhaps changed the way they work. What they do is what you see them doing right now; scrubbing peanut butter out of someone else's hair or singing nursery rhymes on a multicolored carpet. Perhaps it's better to use your children as the meet point, from which you can assess a potential new friend. Watching how another adult plays with their child, talks to them, or even reprimands them is often a good indicator of whether you might be of a like mind. Ask how their night was—all caregivers are obsessed with sleep in the way all medieval kings were obsessed with armor; both are under siege. If you see them out and about in the same places—whether a sandbox or a muse-um—tell them that whatever they're doing looks like fun and see if the compliment opens up a greater dialogue.

From there, with luck and good grace, other things will follow; politics, culture, work, housing, religion, art and Life B.C (before children). A friend-ship may flourish. Perhaps even the sort of friendship that can exist away from the props and struts of your children's company. But it may well be that the only way to look out over the conversational mountain tops with someone new is to slog up the parenting foothills together. So, don't feel embarassed to start another conversation with child talk; the patter of little footprints might just lead somewhere brilliant. k

# — **Gender Agenda**
## Because no child is too young to feel the weight of stereotypes!

For decades, researchers have been tricking adults into revealing the gender biases they hold by disguising the gender of a "baby X" and monitoring how they interact with it. These studies show that not only do adults play differently with "Mary" as opposed to "Johnny," but they even interpret the baby's temperament differently —the same baby might be described as socially engaged when dressed in stereotypically feminine clothes, but angry when dressed in typically masculine ones. Here are some other important studies that show some surprising channels through which gender stereotypes assert themselves at an early age. **k**

PRAISE

Parents praise boys and girls equally, but differently. Just over 24% of praise that boys receive is "process praise." Process praise is important because it rewards a child for their effort and strategies. In comparison, girls receive 10% process praise.

**6**

The age at which girls become significantly less likely than boys to say that girls are "really, really smart."

ABILITY

Mothers of 11-month-old girls estimate that their daughters can crawl down slopes of 14 degrees, whereas mothers of boys believe their sons can crawl down steeper slopes of 20 degrees. In reality, there is no gender difference in crawling ability.

It is important to remember that gender identity should not be projected
onto a child. Some of these studies took place more than a decade ago, and all assume that participating
children's gender identity aligns with the sex they were assigned at birth. Psychology studies also tend to
overrepresent middle-class and white families. (It is not a coincidence that Baby X is typically
given Caucasian names like "Mary" and "Johnny.") See page 119 for a list of reference papers.

# "PARENTS PRAISE BOYS
# AND GIRLS EQUALLY, BUT DIFFERENTLY."

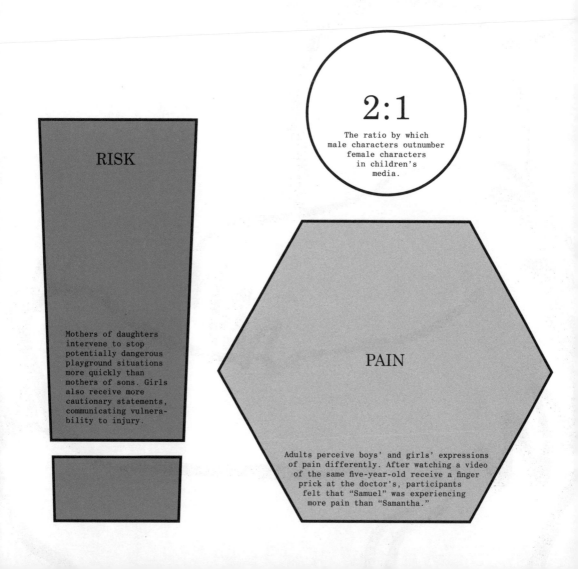

**2:1**

The ratio by which
male characters outnumber
female characters
in children's
media.

RISK

Mothers of daughters
intervene to stop
potentially dangerous
playground situations
more quickly than
mothers of sons. Girls
also receive more
cautionary statements,
communicating vulnera-
bility to injury.

PAIN

Adults perceive boys' and girls' expressions
of pain differently. After watching a video
of the same five-year-old receive a finger
prick at the doctor's, participants
felt that "Samuel" was experiencing
more pain than "Samantha."

Words
TOM WHYMAN

In the first of Julia Donaldson and Axel Scheffler's *Gruffalo* books, published in 1999 and wildly popular ever since, a little mouse is strolling through a deep dark wood, dodging predators as he looks for his dinner. To control the various creatures who threaten him, the mouse manifests the idea of a creature called the gruffalo, as if from the sum of all his fears: a mythic apex predator, a hybrid of all the terrible things one might imagine. The mouse describes the gruffalo to the fox, the owl, the snake… and then poof! The gruffalo actually appears.

Having come to be through fear, fear then becomes the animus of the gruffalo's existence. At the end of the first book, the mouse frightens off the gruffalo by convincing him that he—the mouse—is in fact the scariest creature in the whole of the wood, before stating his intent to eat him. In the 2004 sequel *The Gruffalo's Child*, the gruffalo's life continues to be completely dominated by this encounter. Having been chased from his home, sheltering still terrified in a cave, we learn about the gruffalo as a father. And what does he give to the daughter who has appeared? Nothing, perhaps, save *his own fears*. When his child wants to know why she can't go into the wood, the gruffalo responds:

"Because if you do / The Big Bad Mouse will be after you."

The English novelist Bruce Chatwin speculated that human intelligence originally evolved as a defense mechanism against some grave external threat, so that now, even as we have ascended to become the dominant species on the planet, our brains will continue to invent new threats. Some worries are perfectly justified: I am scared to let my toddler wander into the middle of a busy road, or play unsupervised on the stairs; I am also right to be. But then I have other fears, passed on to me by my own parents perhaps, which only exist to agonize over—and not actually for any good reason. I might know this, at least on some level, but it still imposes a limit on the extent to which my son might discover the world for himself. When I was a child, I was terrified of dogs and remain wary when my son is around them. My fears threaten to make him like myself.

Given this, *The Gruffalo's Child* seems to be teaching us a rather strange lesson. Initially, the gruffalo's warning does not take: bored one night, his child wanders into the wood, in search of the terrible mouse (as any child who has been subject to repeated warnings from their parents that they do not quite understand might do.)

But then she finds him and gets spooked—the mouse's cunning does the trick once more, and her father's irrational fear *seems* justified. When the child returns home, there is something cozy about the scene that unfolds: safe once more, the two gruffalos snuggle up together

## "FEAR IS THE ANIMUS OF THE GRUFFALO'S EXISTENCE."

in their cave. But it is there the story leaves the child: "a little less brave… a bit less bored." A little less curious, in short.

The fear has been passed on to the next generation. Without fear, there need be no such thing as a gruffalo. But here perhaps is the real lesson of the book for parents: *You do not need to be like the gruffalo.* Anxieties may bind us, but they need not bind our children. **k**

Our writer Tom says *The Gruffalo* is one of his son's favorite bedtime stories, although the narrative is sometimes hampered by him closing the book and waving once the animals have said goodbye to the mouse at the beginning.

— **On The Couch**

# What can the gruffalo teach us about inherited fear?

# We attempt to answer the knottiest questions that come with raising—or being—a child.

## — Great Question!

> Question from an adult:
>
> WHY DOES MY CHILD ALWAYS ASK WHY?

I find the timing peculiar. My children find it appealing. During the most breathless moments of family life—while juggling groceries, or jogging the school run—the "Whys?" pour out of them. "Why am I real?" "Why aren't my eyes on my knees?" "Why can't you drive with your neck?" Often, the questions are charming. But once it's apparent that your child has a solid case of The Whys—the desire to ask, without a corresponding desire to be satisfied by the answer—it may feel overwhelming.

Julie Wright, a New York-based child psychotherapist and author, says that there's a "myriad of reasons" why children plow adults with questions. Curiosity is a primary factor, especially between the ages of two and four. As we age and become accustomed to life, we filter out details. Children soak them up. "It's like trying to absorb a whole encyclopedia in one day. They have so many real questions about how things work," she says.

Children may also ask "why" when craving attention, especially if their parent is occupied, or exhibits "interesting" behavior—psychotherapist

shorthand for being distracted or annoyed. Wright's advice is to approach these questions in an empathic and limit-setting way. Let them know that you're listening and trying to understand them. And—if it's a question they've asked a bajillion times before—find a way to reframe the conversation. Children absorb emotion more strongly than we do, but don't have the language skills to express their feelings when scary things or transitions occur. At many points during the COVID-19 pandemic, for example, children asked "Why?" because they could sense the disruption around them but couldn't label it. Arm them with a coherent narrative, Wright advises: "If you give them some language and understanding of whatever it is they may be anxious about, then they don't need to cope with the anxiety."

Wright says that while answering a child in a mindful way may be taxing in the moment, it pays off in the long-term: "When your teenager has a question that's much more important than what your three-year-old is asking, you've established that you take their questions seriously—that you're there to listen and to help." **k**

Words
CHIE DAVIS

Question from
a child:

WHY DO
PEOPLE DIE?

If your child springs this question on you, you can be fairly certain they're not curious about the mechanics of it all: like how your innards slow and ultimately peter out when you get old, no matter how many bowls of muesli you've eaten. No. Your child wants to know why people die at all. Why can't everyone—you, grandpa, that nice lady at the corner shop— just live forever?

There are a number of answers you can give. People die to make room for other people, so that these others can run and play and do all the fun things you like to do (it's a space issue). People die because years are like all good things— like ice cream!—better and more appreciated if we don't gorge ourselves on them. People

die because, well, honey, I'm not sure exactly why they do, but it's okay to feel sad about grandpa dying, because I'm really sad about it, too. People die (for the faithful among you) so that they can go to another, even better place.

What you don't want to do is focus on the negative. "I would shield kids from the hard physical facts of dying," says Dacher Keltner, co-author of *Understanding Emotions.* "And I think you have to stay away from blame—well, she had a drinking problem, that's why she got cancer. You have to treat it more as just a part of life, that this is a shared human experience." And a lot depends on your child's age. "Developmental psychologists would say you have to be really delicate

Words
ROBERT ITO

early, because these are big ideas. And then as kids head into their teens, this is one of the big questions of existence, and you've got to be ready as a parent to take it on."

The main thing to tell your children is that nobody dies, not really, as long as we keep them in our hearts, the way Wilbur did with Charlotte, every time that most amiable of pigs glanced up at the doorway of the barn to watch his friend's tiny spider children, and her children's children, spinning their webs. *Charlotte's Web* is, of course, a first-rate book for kids about death and mourning, even better if they let you read it to them. **k**

In many cultures, the majestic owl is a symbol of death. Turn to page 112 to see some sillier birds. To hear more from Dacher, turn to page 98.

# Staycation supplies for all the family.

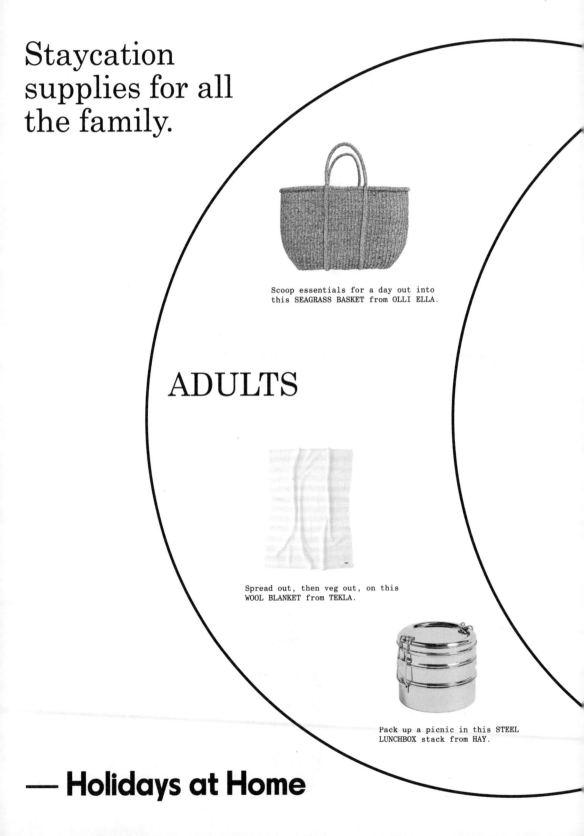

Scoop essentials for a day out into
this SEAGRASS BASKET from OLLI ELLA.

## ADULTS

Spread out, then veg out, on this
WOOL BLANKET from TEKLA.

Pack up a picnic in this STEEL
LUNCHBOX stack from HAY.

## — Holidays at Home

If you're looking for a fun, free holiday activity, turn to page 66 for some DIY fort inspiration.

Learn the Swedish lawn game KUBB. We got this set from BEX SPORT.

Layer up with the NOAM SHIRT from CO LABEL.

# BOTH           KIDS

Become a backyard ornithologist with BIRD BINGO, available at ARKET.

Plan an adventure with the KÅNKEN MINI backpack from FJÄLLRÄVEN.

WELL DONE! You found our cover star CLAUDE. This sweet mascot was knitted by our editor's mum.

Q&A:

# REGINALD DWAYNE BETTS [born **1980**] was only **16** when he was sentenced to nine years in prison for his first offence. Now a poet (also a lawyer, teacher and memoirist) he speaks to *Robyn Price Pierre* about how fatherhood has changed him.

As a teenager, Reginald Dwayne Betts (who goes by Dwayne) was sentenced to nine years in a high-security prison for his involvement in a carjacking in Washington D.C. He started writing poetry in prison, after someone slipped a copy of Dudley Randall's *The Black Poets* under his cell door while in solitary. Since his release in 2005, Dwayne has studied at Yale to become a lawyer, worked on projects to transform access to literature in prisons, and written books and poetry including the acclaimed 2020 collection *Felon*. He lives in New Haven with his wife Terese and their sons Micah and Miles.

**RPP:** Tell me a little bit about your children. What are their names?

**RDB:** We have a nine-year-old named Miles Thelonious and a 13-year-old named Micah Michael Zamir. Micah is a huge reader, and Miles' thing is sports; he loves basketball. And he is a really empathetic kid.

**RPP:** How did you select their names?

**RDB:** My wife's brother— he passed, and his name is Michael. Micah is Michael in Hebrew. I have a line in one of my poems, "Twice named you for the uncle you would never meet." And Miles, you know, Miles Davis.

**RPP:** How does fatherhood show up in your poetry?

**RDB:** I wrote a few poems that touch on it. I think I'm still working through a lot of stuff, although I've been a father for a minute. My kids want to play, and we're like, "You need to do homework!" And then I start remembering that when I was young nobody policed whether or not I was doing my homework. Some of these things become poems, asking questions of what it means to be a father, asking where is the line between being present and being a helicopter parent. But I've only written three, maybe. One about telling my kids about the way in which certain men treat women—sexual assault, sexual violence. And then one about them to just sort of celebrate their birth. And then one about

telling them about the crimes of my past and my time spent in prison.

**RPP:** What is their understanding about your time in prison?

**RDB:** I think now they've just been around it, and it's just a thing. My youngest son will tell me, "I'm sorry you had to go to jail." And my oldest son, after years of listening to me talk about it in different places—on panels, before university students—he understands it in a way that shouldn't be necessary for a 13-year-old. But they know from what I've said or what they've heard. They don't know yet from what they've read. So, I think it will still continue to deepen.

## "WE'RE GOING TO BE SAFE BECAUSE YOU'RE A LAWYER... RIGHT?"

**RPP:** In your poem, *When I think of Tamir Rice While Driving*, about the 12-year-old Black boy killed while playing with a toy gun, you write, "And this is why I hate it all." I won't quote more because I think it needs to be read in its entirety. But as a parent, I know that feeling. Can you share more about that?

**RDB:** My youngest son says all the time, "I was worried about you." When I ask, "Why?" He says, "Well, you know, the police and COVID." So in their way, they really do see it and think about it. He'll say things like, "We're going to be safe from the police... because you're a lawyer. Right?" But I think the thing that disgusts me about all of it is we live in these competing moments where you're supposed to say you're a [prison] abolitionist and also pretend like you aren't enraged by the complicated ways that crime and violence have come to mark the lives of so many Black folks in this country.

I just find it both heartbreaking and overwhelmingly infuriating. And at the end of the day, I grapple with *how come the response is always peace?* I wrote that poem because I had given somebody else a prompt: "Write a poem that you won't let anybody else read." And then I wrote it, and I didn't think I was ever going to let somebody read it. And then I got so mad in law school one day that I sent it to the whole law school. I was like, fuck it. I didn't even have a comment. No preamble. I just sent it.

**RPP:** In what ways are your children growing up differently than you did? I imagine there is a different level of access and privilege.

**RDB:** I always think what matters most, really, is that I've been an artist. I don't work in

# "WHERE IS THE LINE BETWEEN BEING PRESENT AND BEING A HELICOPTER PARENT?"

big law. I've been home, most of the time. When our oldest was born, me and my wife were both going into our junior year of undergrad. We both worked full time, but our schedules were just way more flexible than the traditional nine to five. There are other ways in which it's different based on having two parents that have graduate degrees. My wife is an occupational therapist. And they know what that is. My sons are a part of and hear conversations that expose them to different professions, different spaces, different ways of being. It just gives them a different set of tools to imagine and engage with the world. Yeah, I'm a lawyer and maybe that gives them a little bit of, "Oh, my dad's a lawyer." But they don't care about that, because their friend's parents are all *something*. And most of their friends are from two-parent households. You kind of take it for granted. Growing up,

I didn't think of it as a "thing." And I'm still not certain how much I think of it as a "thing" now. But it's real. I've had hard times. My wife has had hard times. And it's something meaningful for one of them to have constant attention, for one of us to be able to cook dinner while the other one relaxes, or does school work, or does "work work." It's real, you know, the life we've been able to build. So I would say their daily lives differ from mine for a lot of reasons. And maybe Yale is one of them. And maybe I push back on that because I'm still not whatever typical "Yale" is.

**RPP:** What have you learned from your kids?

**RDB:** My son once said, "Daddy, I'm different from my classmates." My first response is, "What? You're different? I have a Yale law degree too! Your classmates' parents haven't written these books. I'm in *The New York Times*. Where they

at? And he is like, "Well, what I'm saying is they don't have to walk around in a world knowing their dad carjacked somebody." One of the things they teach me pretty consistently is that if your only understanding of incarceration is what the latest celebrity abolitionist says, you'll forget how painful it is to know that someone you love hurt somebody else. My son isn't tripping off prison as much as the fact that I held a pistol to somebody's head. And one of the things they teach me is that what you do matters. We think about incarceration and what the state does. But they teach me a lot about the fact that what we do matters. And I think that's the most important thing. **k**

You can find a longer version of Dwayne and Robyn's conversation on our website.

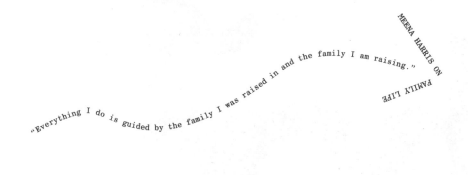

"Everything I do is guided by the family I was raised in and the family I am raising."

MEENA HARRIS ON
FAMILY LIFE

Big
Reads

# meena
# harris

On raising daughters within the

mother
of
all
matriarchies.

# "Are you proud of your mommy?"

# "Yeah!"

At her home in San Francisco, Meena Harris's four-year-old daughter smiles as she jumps into her mother's lap. I notice a momentary tenseness pass over Meena's face: the familiar act of maintaining a professional demeanor in front of both a journalist and a small person for whom her presence means a warm hug, a kiss, and breakfast for a hungry belly.

Still, as someone whose children are very present in her public life, Meena has had more practice than most. Mother to two girls, a four-year-old and a three-year-old, she is a lawyer, the founder and CEO of lifestyle brand Phenomenal and, most recently, the *New York Times* bestselling author of two children's books: *Kamala and Maya's Big Idea* and *Ambitious Girl*.

Her daughters are looking up at a long line of matriarchs. Meena's mother, Maya Harris, is an American lawyer and public policy advocate, who was one of the senior advisors to Hillary Clinton during her 2016 presidential campaign. Her aunt, Kamala Harris is the first Black and Asian woman to become Vice President of the USA. The lineage goes back further, to their mother, Shyamala Gopalan, a biomedical scientist who moved from Chennai to Berkeley, California, in 1958. "My grandmother came to the United States and became deeply involved in the Civil Rights movement," says Meena, who describes Shyamala as a "second mother" to her growing up. "But that was not where her identity or ideology came from. It came from her family in India. My great grandfather was a diplomat—this was in her DNA. It was no surprise that she made a choice to identify with the struggle."

Born into this matriarchy in 1984, Meena has been boosted by its prestige. "Everyone in my family has had a public profile in some way," she says. "I had an understanding of the public or *external* in a way that other people

who don't have families like that would." Still, she has not moved ahead without doing the work. She obtained her B.A. from Stanford University and is a Harvard Law graduate. Did she feel pressure to go to law school? "I can't frame it as pressure," she says. "That's all that I knew." As a younger woman, the thing that did occasionally cause strain was her awareness of how public-facing the women in her family were: "I was too concerned with external validation or what I thought people would see to be impressive," she says.

Growing up, Meena had a front-row seat to watch the women in her family achieve their goals. Maya Harris was 17 years old and a single mother when she had her daughter, but she continued to pursue her dreams. Meena would accompany her mom to work and was proud to witness her obtain her college and law degrees. "These things impacted me in a meaningful way," she says. Maya went on to become the youngest law school dean in the country.

Above: Meena wears a sweater by PRADA and earrings by JENNIFER FISHER.

One of Meena's goals with her own daughters is to teach them to be appreciative of their own privilege. "It's hard when you have new privileges. You know what it's like not having them and how it contributes to raising good kids who have work ethic so that they can appreciate things," she says. This is the odd tension that comes with having achieved the sort of life that you want for your child: we hope to raise them to not have to experience the struggles of our own childhood, and yet we want them to have the same appreciation for life that those struggles gave us. She says hand me downs are still a thing in their household.

"It's hard when you have new privileges.
You know what it's like not having them
and how it contributes to raising good kids
who can appreciate things."

Meena now encourages her children to be a part of work events. She is aware of the impact of her girls seeing their mother outside of her normative role of parent. One of the most memorable events her daughter joined was a Mother's Day pop-up hosted by Phenomenal. "My youngest daughter was only three months old!" she says with excitement. For Meena, her family life flourishes by providing her daughters with examples of following your dreams. "There are trade-offs," she says. "When you are talking about [mom] guilt, you have to reframe that. It is good for girls and boys to see women working and women believing. It contributes to our children's views of seeing women doing what men have always done. This is not something that should be hidden or taken away from parenting."

Meena wears a top, skirt and shoes by PRADA, and jewelry by JENNIFER FISHER.

During women's history month in 2017, Meena launched what would become her lifestyle brand Phenomenal with a simple T-shirt that read *Phenomenal Woman*. "Phenomenal was supposed to be a one-month side project," she says. After immediately seeing what an impact the brand was capable of having—it sold 2,500 T-shirts on its first day—she realized it would bypass its one-month initiative. Meena started launching more slogan T-shirts and supporting humanitarian causes like Higher Heights, The Breona Taylor Foundation, This Is About

Humanity, and Native Voices Rising, as well as designing personalized campaigns in allyship with social issues such as pay equity for women of color and ending family separation at the border. One of Phenomenal's most impressive mobilizations was lobbying 1,600 men to sign their names to a letter in support of Christine Blasey Ford, the professor and research psychologist who alleged she was assaulted in 1982 by Brett Kavanaugh, Donald Trump's nominee to the Supreme Court. Through the efforts of organizations including Phenomenal, $100,000 was raised to take out a full-page ad in *The New York Times* in September 2018 pledging solidarity with her. These are all campaigns that put pay to the comments she received online when she first started the business: namely that she was wasting her Harvard Law degree to "make T-shirts."

For Meena, Phenomenal is a final break with the "traditional path" of her family, although one that's informed by the advantages that family has granted her. "It's a huge privilege to decide you will go and do your own thing," she says. "Having a Harvard Law degree helped me not just develop essential skills that allowed me to be successful in what I do, but also having that credential, having that credibility as a woman of color, doing something that I had never done before." As she puts it more bluntly: "I would love to see a world where women of color don't need a fucking law degree on top of a good idea to be able to succeed."

Meena wears a top by NANUSHKA, trousers by THE FRANKIE SHOP, earrings by JENNIFER FISHER and her own BIRKENSTOCKS.

"Everything I do is guided by the family I was raised in and the family that I am raising now."

When Phenomenal launched, Meena had given birth nine months prior. The business grew with her motherhood. Publishing was a logical next step. "A lot of what we do through Phenomenal is around storytelling," says Meena. "Children's books are yet another medium in which we can do that." In the summer of 2020, she published *Kamala and Maya's Big Idea*. The book focuses on the true story of her mother and aunt turning their apartment courtyard into a playground that all the children in the neighborhood could enjoy. It's a story of perseverance and adversity, intended to inspire young girls to turn their own dreams into reality. This year, she's written the follow-up *Ambitious Girl*. Once again inspired by the matriarchs in her family, she wanted to change the narrative that she was constantly hearing in the media— that the Harris women were too ambitious. Meena reflects on the emotions that washed over her the first time she read *Ambitious Girl* with her daughters. "It's really extraordinary. I am just amazed at how kids soak these things up and how it affects them and impacts them."

The books are an attempt to spread the ethos that she grew up with. "I can attest to that constantly circulating in my household," she says. "Everything I do is guided by the family I was raised in and the family that I am raising now. It went from memorializing this family story to share with my kids to discovering there's a huge issue of lack of diversity in the publishing industry and kid's books."

These are industry-changing achievements, but for Meena the current meaning of "phenomenal" lands closer to home. "We've had a lot happen over the last two years." She laughs. "Phenomenal means doing the dishes and folding clothes. It means our family being safe and healthy. I obviously have big dreams and aspirations but today I'm just taking it day by day."

Whatever she does next, her daughters will be by her side. "My oldest daughter is now four and I have vivid memories of accompanying my mother [to work] at that age," she says. "For now, she is having fun crashing my Zoom meetings." k

Our writer Shanicia says that Meena jokingly compared her family situation to the opening scenes of *Wonder Woman*, set in an all-female sovereign nation.

# A WORLD AWAY:

*Elle Hunt* considers
        the realities of traveling with
children and reflects on her own
        four years at sea.

For four years of my childhood, my family and I lived on board a yacht. Sailing the world had been my dad's dream since he was in his 20s, later embraced by my mom. My younger sister Jess and I grew up in Dorset anticipating our departure, allowed only hamsters because longer-lasting pets would clash with "The Trip."

When we eventually set out from Weymouth Marina in May 2000, having sold our house and most of our possessions, Jess was seven years old and I was nine. Our longest unbroken stint at sea was three weeks; we did that twice. But most of the time we island-hopped between some of the world's most desirable honeymoon destinations (Barbados, Bora Bora) and islands so remote (the Marquesas, the Tuamotus) they could only be accessed by sea.

As much as it was my parents' lifelong dream, it was also our daily life. My mum, a teacher, homeschooled Jess and I. Fixing things—more often than not, it seemed, the sewage holding tank—became my dad's full-time job. And for four years, we were very rarely more than 52 feet apart, which started to grate on me the closer I got to puberty. Though we had planned to return to the UK, we eventually settled in Nelson, New Zealand. My parents returned to work and Jess and I reentered the school system. In hindsight, it is remarkable how easy it was to pick back up on normal life—much easier than it was to let go of it.

My experience has made me curious about the kind of people who choose to lead unconventional lives with children. Though young families are relatively unusual among "cruisers" (most sailors attempt their circumnavigation in retirement), it is not uncommon to hear of parents pulling their children out of school to travel for 12 months or more. Indeed, it is becoming more popular as first-person accounts on blogs and social media make taking a family "gap year" or longer-term "world schooling" seem not only desirable—but possible.

"More people are aware now that you can," says Alyson Long, over Zoom from her Brisbane home. "It's not a fringe thing." Long set up WorldTravelFamily.com in 2012 to share updates from the round-the-world trip she took with her husband when their sons were six and eight years old. When the blog found a vast audience of parents wanting to follow suit, Long developed it into a practical resource. The advertising revenue enabled the Longs to extend their trip to six years of full-time travel. Now relatively settled in Australia, Long remains a point of contact

Interviewing other traveling families for *Kindling* made Elle reflect on how "The Trip" that her own family took has shaped her personality. "The older I get, the smaller a proportion of my life those years on the boat becomes, but it's still such a big part of who I am," she says.

"It is remarkable how easy it was to pick back up on

for families curious about leading a no-madic life, the increasing traffic to her site testament to their number. (And their demographics: Long's readers tend to be well-educated women over 35.) She esti-mates that there are tens of thousands of families actively planning their departure, even during a pandemic.

Much of Long's website is dedicated to busting the myth that you have to be a millionaire to go globe-trotting. One year's (certainly budget-conscious) travel for her family of four cost $30,000: "We did the maths and it was cheaper to travel than it was to stay here," she says. Her analy-sis of other round-the-world families put the average cost of 12 months of travel at $20,000 per person, though it could vary dramatically according to the destination, mode of transport and individual threshold for "roughing it."

As much as a "family yacht" may be shorthand for wealth, it took both my parents years of saving to afford the trip; for four years we lived frugally, mostly in countries with a low cost of living (and few opportunities to spend). After The Trip was over, they went back to work. Twenty years later, internet access has improved and work has become more flexible, making it possible for more people—although only those in white-collar professions—to main-tain a regular income as "digital nomads."

Even among those of comparable oppor-tunity, not everyone will aspire to lead a no-madic lifestyle. Parents who are mindful of their carbon footprint will have legitimate reservations about extended travel. And if

you are deeply rooted in your work, local community or extended family, the idea might hold no appeal. "It is a big commit-ment, and a big responsibility... which a lot of other people aren't happy to do," says Long. "That's totally fair enough." Long has noticed that a lot of "long-termers" are couples of mixed nationalities, like hers: "I think there's an element of *nowhere is really home*."

Equally, the experience won't suit every child. "If you pull a very sociable child out of school, they're going to hate it, proba-bly," says Long. Her advice is to "know your kids... Some are just going to shut down and be resentful." Indeed, my own mount-ing difficulty with boat life as a 12-year-old was one reason my family stopped traveling.

But among those families with the where-withal and the desire to travel, put off only by the seemingly insurmountable obsta-cles, Long's message is: It may be more pos-sible than you think. Today, what strikes me most about my parents' decision is just that: It was a decision, then a series of steps. In 2010, Melissa Wiringi was solo-parenting her two small children when she heard about a round-the-world family from a friend. "It really touched something in me," Wiringi tells me. "It was like: *I want to do this*."

Growing up in Rotorua, a relatively small town in New Zealand, Wiringi had seen the harm that could come from feel-ing trapped by your circumstances. It was a factor in her own abusive relationship, she says. Wiringi wanted her children to grow up empowered, able to feel at home anywhere in the world.

normal life—much easier than it was to let go of it."

The clincher was discovering Long's blog years later, when she was living in Australia with her new husband. Wiringi learned that what they had spent on a five-week holiday in Europe had supported the Longs for a year. In 2015, they began working towards their dream of full-time travel, persevering through pregnancy, injury and redundancy.

At long last, their family of five departed in March 2020—first stop, Vietnam. When we spoke toward the end of the year, they were still there, their plans disrupted by COVID-19. Still, the time has been transformative says Wiringi over WhatsApp: "I'd spent months with my spreadsheet. Throwing that out the window has made me a different person."

Her children, now four, 12 and 13, have become confident explorers of their new surroundings. The older two, who had struggled with mainstream schooling, are motivated to invest in their interests. "In the real world they're going to thrive," says Wiringi. More important to her is that her children are learning to be "who they are"—outside their comfort zone, but supported by their family unit.

Long believes her sons feel more capable as a result of their six years spent traveling, the obstacles (not least, frequent boredom) as influential as the opportunities. "I just think they're going to think unconventionally, see more possibilities in the world, not be afraid to go after different things," she says. But the flip side of feeling a connection to the world, Long acknowledges, is that it may lead her boys away from her. "They don't have strong roots."

I see that at play in my own family, scattered more often than not. It is telling that we have not spent Christmas together in six years. But I also recognize in myself the single-mindedness that Long praises in her sons. It was on the boat that I discovered my love for writing, after I'd run out of books to read. Having weathered storms and scaled mountains in childhood, my sister and I don't balk at a challenge as adults. And though I may be no sailor myself, those long weeks at sea turned out to be excellent prep for lockdown. But my biggest takeaway from childhood was that I could take charge of my future, my parents' decision to lead an unconventional life at sea opening my mind to possibilities in my own—on land. **k**

Elle remembers that the islands of the South Pacific were the most child-friendly out of all the places her family visited (despite being marketed in the West as honeymoon destinations). "Empty golden beaches and teeming coral reefs are playgrounds for a child."

# THROW

One bed sheet, two tin cans and three children—a homespun stage for adventure.

SH
APES

Jeremy wears a
T-shirt and pants
by INDUSTRY OF ALL
NATIONS, a shirt
by MISHA & PUFF
and shoes by DR.
MARTENS. Nalani
wears a sweater
by MISHA & PUFF,
overalls by MOLO,
the stylist's socks
and shoes by MABO.

Previous page: Jeremy wears a T-shirt by INDUSTRY OF ALL NATIONS, a shirt by MISHA & PUFF, and a jacket and trousers by NOBLE CARRIAGE. Nalani wears a top and trousers by MOLO, and cardigans by OEUF and ZARA. Daphne wears a T-shirt by MOLO, a turtleneck by FIN & VINCE, and trousers by PARACHUTE BROOKLYN.

Daphne wears a turtleneck by FIN & VINCE, and a vest by MISHA & PUFF. Our photographer Oumayma says Daphne had some great dance moves on set.

Daphne wears a
turtleneck by FIN
& VINCE. Turn the
page to see what
she's looking at!

KIDS' CORNER:
You only need a
torch and a bed-
sheet to make your
own shadow show!

Hair: EROL KARADAĞ Makeup: AYAKA NIHEI Casting: NOURI HASSAN Production: CAROLIN RAMSAUER at Abovo Management
Photo Assistants: AMELIA HAMMOND, JORDI PEREZ Styling Assistant: JAMES KELLEY
Models: DAPHNE & JEREMY at Generation Model Management, NALANI at New York Models

Nalani wears a
turtleneck by FIN &
VINCE, a jumpsuit
by NOBLE CARRIAGE,
a sweater by BABAÀ,
the stylist's
socks, and shoes by
BONPOINT.

Jeremy wears a
turtleneck by FIN
& VINCE, a sweater
by MISHA & PUFF,
trousers by NOBLE
CARRIAGE, shoes
by BONPOINT and
the stylist's
necklace and socks.
Not pictured: the
inside of Jeremy's
mouth, dyed red
from eating a
lot of cherry
STARBURSTS during
this shoot.

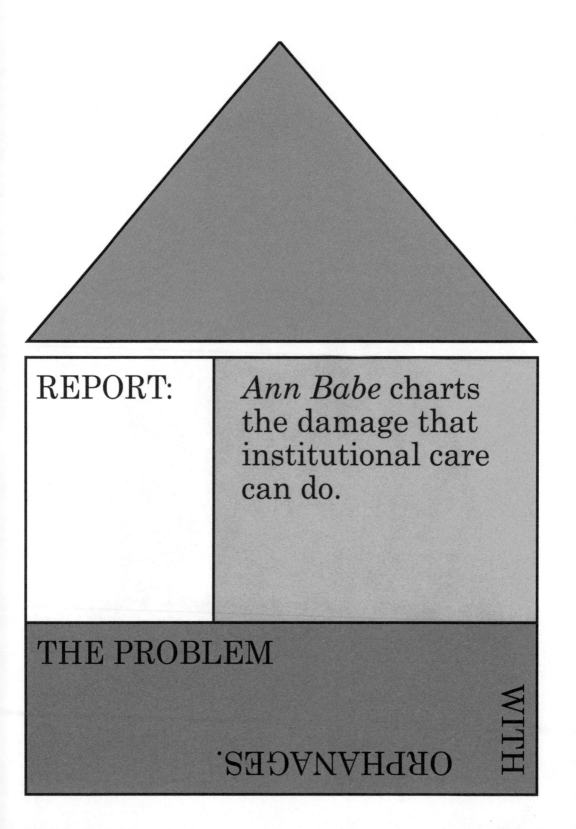

REPORT:

*Ann Babe* charts the damage that institutional care can do.

THE PROBLEM

ORPHANAGES.

WITH

In 2006, the year that Nepal's decade-long civil war came to an end, three Australian friends founded an orphanage in Kathmandu for girls who had lost their parents to the violence. Registered as an Australian charity, the Forget Me Not children's home started by housing six girls, which soon grew to 20, all of whom had been orphaned by the bloody armed conflict.

Except they hadn't.

As it turned out, none of the girls who lived at the Forget Me Not home were orphans. Their parents were not among the 17,000 dead.

What had occurred was actually an elaborate, yet common, child trafficking scheme, whereby children are actively displaced to orphanages for profit. The Australians were an easy target, their good intentions but severe lack of experience a direct conduit to other well-intentioned but inexperienced people around the world—along with their millions of dollars in donations.

Recruiters had gone to remote villages and made false promises to mothers and fathers. "We'll take your kids to the city for a better education, a better life!" they were told. "It'll just cost a fee." The parents couldn't read what they were signing off on with their thumbprints. The traffickers then forged certificates verifying they were dead. The girls were sold to a corrupt local NGO. For years, the children kept their mouths shut for fear of retribution, until one day they shared their secret with the Forget Me Not country director. The Australians were stunned.

"These 20 little girls were in our orphanage… Their faces were on our Christmas tree, on our magnets on the fridge," recalls Andrea Nave, the CEO of Forget Me Not, which today is dedicated to removing children from institutional care and reuniting them with family. "When this truth came out, I went [to the orphanage]. These little cheeks that I had cupped for years, loving them and rightly or wrongly selling their image to try and generate more funds."

They looked up at her and said, "Please, Auntie, I want to go home."

Worldwide, the number of parentless children is decreasing, but the number of orphanages has been increasing. This rise, according to the children's rights organization ECPAT International, coincides with the popularity of voluntourism, whereby travelers pay to spend a bit of their dream vacation volunteering in an orphanage setting.

OUR WRITER: Ann Babe was adopted from South Korea to the United States as a child. She is now based in South Korea, where she works as an independent journalist writing long-form narratives about the Korean Peninsula and the lives of women.

To make voluntourist access easy, orphanages are often located in tourist areas, a short jaunt away from luxury hotels, cultural attractions and fusion restaurants. When international tourism to Cambodia boomed from 2005 to 2010, so too did its number of orphanages, surging by 75%, according to a 2011 government study. Some of the most startling figures come out of Uganda, where between 1992 and 2013, reports the Faith to Action Initiative, the number of children's homes grew from 30 to 800.

Of the estimated two to eight million children living in orphanages today—numbers range, as verifiable data is impossible to come by—a vast majority are not orphans at all. Around 85% have at least one living parent, according to Save the Children. As Forget Me Not's Kate van Doore put it to *Christianity Today* writer Krish Kandiah in 2019: "Orphanages do not exist because orphans exist. Rather, orphans exist because orphanages exist." Oblivious volunteers leave their orphanage placements aglow with the satisfaction that they've given back to the community they visited. What they don't realize is that they've upheld a system that makes children more valuable when separated from their families than when kept together with them.

"Even the best run orphanages cause harm."

Even the best-run orphanages cause harm. "There are better and worse orphanages," one Save the Children representative told Kandiah, "but there is no such thing as a good orphanage." Again and again, research has proven this to be true. Children in institutions, particularly those who enter at a young age, are more likely to be physically and neurologically stunted than those raised by families or foster families, with one study showing that for every 2.6 months spent in an orphanage, one month of development is lost. They're left with worse motor skills and lower IQs. And over half of those who ever spend any amount of time in an orphanage go on to develop a mental health problem, compared to 22% of the general population.

Experts argue that children under five should never be kept in institutional care. It can be deadly, according

KOREA: The brutal legacy of Western imperialism sits at the root of many orphanage systems. South Korea started sending children overseas for adoption following the violence of the Korean War—the first conflict of the Cold War.

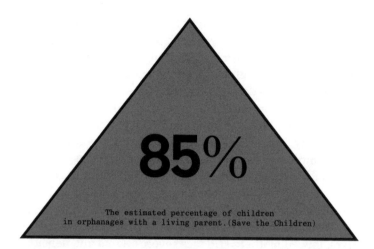

**85%**

The estimated percentage of children
in orphanages with a living parent.(Save the Children)

to Maia Szalavitz, the author of the book *Born for Love:
Why Empathy Is Essential and Endangered*. When a baby
doesn't receive enough physical affection, a necessary
stimulant of the immune system, Szalavitz writes, their
body begins to shut down.

Children's rights groups, national governments and
intergovernmental organizations around the world have
recognized such dangers. The Australian government for-
mally identifies orphanage trafficking as a form of modern slavery. The UK warns its citizens in an official travel
advisory of the harm of orphanage tourism. And the anti-
slavery movement Freedom United runs a campaign call-
ing on tour operators to stop offering volunteer placements
at children's homes.

Decrees and documentation aside, though, deep down,
all of us already know that no orphanage is a truly safe
place for children—because, after all, if something should
happen to you, would you want your child to be put in one?

The original voluntourist might well be considered the
missionary, who introduced the concept of the orphanage
to places that never could have imagined such a thing; it
didn't make sense within societies that used community
care. One such place was the Korean Peninsula. In 1885,
Catholic missionaries from France founded the first Korean orphanage, located in Seoul and big enough to house
400 children. Within a year, they opened another in Dae-
gu. Protestant missionaries came too, and built more orphanages. By 1969, over 15 years after the Korean War,
the number of children's homes had reached its peak, with
more than 540 scattered across South Korea, a country
smaller than the US state of Pennsylvania.

HAITI:
As of 2017,
orphanages
were receiving
$100m a year
in foreign
donations;
130 times the
budget of
country's child
protection
agency.

To understand what might become of Uganda or Cambodia or Haiti if orphanages keep popping up at breakneck speed, one might take a look at what's already happened to South Korea. Though the country has joined the ranks of the world's richest economies, its GDP measuring twelfth, it continues to operate more than 200 children's homes.

Where I'm based, in a midsized city in central South Korea, my life of lightning-fast internet connections, app-summoned taxis and same-day deliveries is backdropped by the orphanage I once lived in, 30 minutes away, nestled amid the farm fields beyond the mountains. When I'm near it, I think about how it is that a nation that's advanced so much could also have progressed so little. Here, unwed mothers still face severe stigma and deficient welfare, leading three in four to relinquish their children, according to one single mothers' association. Children in institutional care still outnumber children in foster care.

The irony, though, is that South Korea has itself become a top missionary sender, supporting orphanages all around the world. But as a donor of humanitarian aid that still relies on humanitarian aid to raise its own children, South Korea demonstrates the real problem with orphanages—that by their very design, they perpetuate themselves, and, in effect, social inaction. What was once a stopgap has since become a stubborn stumbling block to structural change.

Orphanages have become so entrenched that governments often treat them as the first option, not a last resort, diverting money, time and attention away from the more complex but crucial work of tackling the root socioeconomic causes of family separation. This isn't because institutional care is cost-effective—analysis shows it's six

GUATEMALA: A 2018 investigation by *The Guardian* found that foreigners paid up to $1000 for a week of voluntourism. Joining a "baby rescue" cost $500 extra.

"Deep down, we know that no orphanage

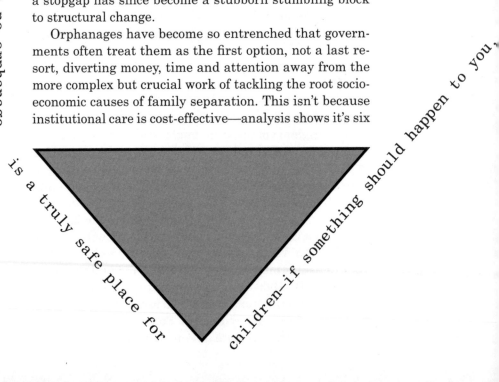

is a truly safe place for children—if something should happen to you,

# 8,000,000

The high estimate of the number of children living in institutions
around the world. (UNICEF)

times more expensive than providing vulnerable parents
with the social support they need in order to keep their
kids, and three times more expensive than professional
foster care—but because institutional care is convenient.

Children's rights organizations say that to end orphanage overuse and misuse, political leaders, NGOs
and faith-based groups must prioritize the prevention of
family breakdowns and redirect resources toward reform,
and donors must invest accordingly. If parental care is
impossible, they add, even despite proper welfare services, then children should be raised in a family setting—
such as kinship care, foster care, adoptive care, or, if a
sibling is old enough, a youth-headed household—not in
an orphanage.

would you want your child to be put in one?"

Lumos, a non-profit headquartered in London, part-
ners with governments and civil society organizations in
Haiti, Colombia, Kenya, Ethiopia and countries across
Eastern Europe to reduce the number of children in orphanages and facilitate family-based care. Another British non-profit, Hope and Homes for Children, works with
leaders in more than 20 nations to eliminate institutional
care systems, one shuttered orphanage at a time. And the
US-based 1MILLIONHOME is committed to transforming
5,000 orphanages into family reunification centers.

Back in Nepal in 2012, the Forget Me Not founders
dismantled the children's home they'd opened only eight
years earlier. And after months of trekking through hills
and valleys—passing around pictures and asking, "Do you
know her parents?"—charity workers were finally able to
send home the 20 girls of the Forget Me Not orphanage,
who, indeed, had never been forgotten. **k**

Fantastic forts
 and how to build them.

CRIB
SH
EETS

UP THE MOUNTAIN:
Create a web of
string attached
to stable points
around the room.
Place sheets over
them and attach
them with pegs and
more string.

Previous Spread:
THE CASTLE:
Use two chairs
to create the
structure for
your castle, then
tie a length of
string between
them. Attach a
broom to the back
of each chair,
and string a line
between the two.
Cover liberally
with sheets.

THE TUNNEL:
Use a tall floor
lamp or garden
canes to create
the peak of the
mountain, then
lie dining
chairs on the
floor to elongate
the tunnel.

Opposite page:
THE TEPEE:
Use garden canes to
create a pyramid
structure, and
secure it in place
with string or
elastic bands.
Cover with sheets.
If you're short on
space at home, the
tepee is a perfect
hidey-hole.

# NATURE
## FOR NURTURE:

If you go down to
        the woods today... you might
learn a thing or two.

Standing in a muddy patch of Oxfordshire woodland, the air milky with early morning mist, a group of children are holding pieces of willow almost twice their height and chanting: "Over and under, over and under."

Huge lengths of willow whip through the sky. One child has a stripe of mud right up one leg, another is still wearing his bike helmet, a third has a suspicious beard of crumbs across his chin. They are weaving; a wreath, a crown, the beginnings of a basket, who knows what exactly. But they are also learning dexterity, a whole new vocabulary, how to share resources, and being encouraged to describe the smell, sound and feel of the wood. They are learning about resistance, kinetic energy, prepositions and, particularly in the case of the girl with mud up her leg, resilience.

The popularity of outdoor learning has soared in recent years, with forest schools —outdoor learning experiences led by specially trained teachers—popping up like mushrooms all over Europe, the US, and from South Korea to Trinidad. In the UK, where I live, the Forest School Association counts more than 2,000 members. The movement has its roots in Scandinavian countries, where it is collectively called *friluftsliv*, a word coined by the Norwegian poet Henrik Ibsen that translates literally as "open-air living." In Sweden, after the founding of the Skogsmulle school network in 1957, the *I Ur Och Skur* (meaning "rain and shine") tradition has encouraged young children to learn outdoors all year round. The Metsämuori school in Finland, the *friluftsbarnehage* in Norway and *åbørnspædagogik* in Denmark all followed soon after and have been frontrunners in bringing child-centered learning outside and into nature.

While formal forest schools sometimes have long waiting lists, or are otherwise inaccessible, the mentality behind the movement translates across time zones and climates, age groups and economic brackets. Due to measures against COVID-19, many families spent more of the last year out in nature than ever before; climbing trees, wading through streams, even just searching for leaves and bugs in a local park.

For parents, forest schooling means creating an environment in which safe, explorative and challenging activities can take place, and then, rather than teaching through example or by rote, allowing their children to take the reins. "We have

Our writer Nell says her son has become obsessed with archery since watching Disney's *Robin Hood*, and they now always take a ball of string and scissors along on outdoor adventures. A bendy wood, like willow, is perfect for making a strong bow.

an expression in Forest School," says instructor Hamish Bennett, as we follow the little band of outdoor weavers through a patch of British woodland. "You are there to be on tap, not on top. That means the kids are meant to lead their own learning and you can just interject occasionally to say 'Ooh, what about this?' or 'Why do you think that's like that?' But if they're enjoying it, you can leave them to it." Bennett, who is rarely out of shorts, smiles as one of the troop gets snared on an overhanging bramble. "Even as a forest school teacher, I'm naturally quite risk-averse," he says, untangling their sleeve. "So I have to remind myself to let them get on with it. I think it's great for children to get dirty, maybe wet and cold. To learn about getting warm through your own exertion."

You do not necessarily have to sign up to a formal forest school or outdoor learning organization to reap the benefits of the movement. There are plenty of small and easy activities to start with that can build a love of outdoor exploration for little ones. Collecting things to study, for instance, often takes little more equipment than some old mason jars. Journey sticks[*] are a great way to encourage narrative development and observation skills; simply wrap a stick in string and then push the things you find along the way—feathers, flowers, seeds, grasses, leaves—under the loops. By the end, you will have a tiny totem pole of finds, which children can use to tell the story of their walk. Alternatively, you can take a piece of cardboard, cover it with patches of double-sided tape and then stick the things you find to the board, as a display. The aim is to describe how those things look, smell, move and sound, rather than simply naming them and moving on. In some ways, this is where the practice of outdoor learning can intersect with

"Outdoor learning can intersect with mindfulness; encouraging children to have a deeper, sensory relationship with their environment."

* Journey sticks were first used by Indigenous communities in Australia and North America. The sequential addition of objects found over the course of long journeys meant that the stick could later be used as a memory prompt—both for story telling, and to help people retrace their steps.

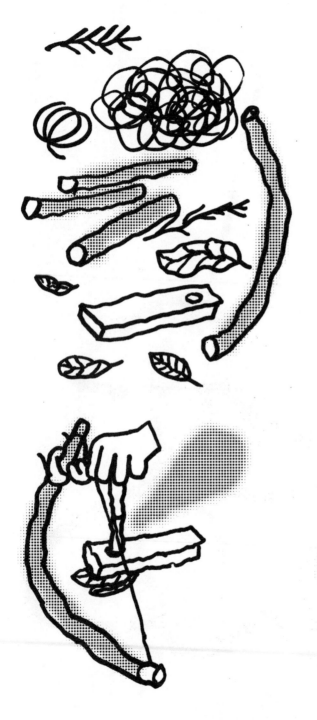

"You are there to be on tap,
          not on top. If they're enjoying it,
   you can leave them to it."

mindfulness; encouraging children to have a deeper, sensory relationship with their environment in the moment.

Leaf boats are a simple and equipment-free way to learn about buoyancy, surface tension and weight. If outdoor access is difficult, they can float in a puddle or a sink. The simplest way of making a boat is to push the stem of the leaf through its tip so it turns into a little leaf curl, which can float on water. However, you can also use big, flat leaves as sails by threading them onto a stick and then pushing the end of that stick into a carved hole in a piece of bark or flattish piece of wood, to act like the hull. Even if it doesn't float, it's an opportunity for an interesting conversation. "It's about child-led learning," explains Bennett. "You can add different elements to their play to help them move along, or do something they want to do."

Fire is possibly the greatest magnet for children when it comes to outdoor learning, and one of the most exciting challenges.

The bow fire technique, which has been used by Indigenous communities for thousands of years, is an extremely physical way to make fire from scratch—a great activity on cold days. You will need four basic elements: the drill, the hearth, a bearing block and the bow. The drill will be a piece of branch, the end of which sits in the hearth—a carved dip in a flat piece of dry wood. You will then need to make the bow, which is essentially a piece of string or rope strung between the two ends of a curved stick. To light a fire, wrap the bow's string in a loop around your drill, so that when you move the bow from side to side, the drill spins against the hearth. You will need to apply some pressure to the top of the drill, which is where the bearing block comes in. Eventually, and with enough friction, the hearth will start to char and smoke. If you tap enough of these charred embers into a pile of very dry leaves or grass and blow on it, you should get flames leaping up from the bundle. "You definitely come across all sorts of

" When you're outdoors, there's something
called soft fascination. It's where all your senses are
stimulated in lots of different ways at once;
touch, smell, sound, sight."

things from the early years curriculum in outdoor learning," says Bennett. He strings a piece of rope over a high branch, ties the other end around a large piece of wood and, hey presto, a swing has appeared to be fought over by the children. "Counting, building shapes, estimating, finding different units of measurement like handspan, wingspan and foot length... You can also learn about leverage with digging or using a stick to move a large, heavy stone. Friction and air resistance are quite nice things to experiment with outside; throwing feathers to see how they fall, dragging big light objects versus smaller, heavier objects to see which is harder. I brought my daughter here the other day," he says, gesturing toward a fire pit near a pond. "There was charcoal leftover from a fire, so we were just looking at it, feeling it, using it to make marks and talking about the moss around it." As children get older and more confident there is a world of natural navigation, fire cooking, log splitting and tree climbing to enjoy. All for free and usually with very little equipment. "When you're outdoors, there's something called soft fascination", explains Bennett, cutting off a length of ivy and showing one of the mud-splattered children at our shins how to weave it into their willow creations. "It's where all your senses are stimulated in lots of different ways at once; touch, smell, sound, sight... Soft fascination is very calming and helps you to focus more because you can find your own way."

Walking back through the willow trees to a patch of grass, the mist almost dissipated, the mud on our legs almost dry, one of the knee-height weavers drops to the floor and grabs a snail shell, hooting with delight. "It's a fossil!" he shouts. "It's treasure!" shouts another. "I think it might be magic," says the third. They are in their element. They are learning. They are having fun. **k**

79 — 104

# Emotions

Raindrops on roses and
whiskers on kittens,
bright copper kettles

# hap
# py
# child.

and warm
woolen
mittens...

# ...brown paper packages tied up with string— a happy child is a recent thing.

London's Victoria and Albert Museum of Childhood is currently undergoing a major refurbishment. The aim, according to senior curator Alex Newson, is to transform the institution into "the most joyful museum in the world." The building will be redesigned to offer elements of delight and surprise, and the exhibits will encourage creativity through interaction and exploration.

The exact form of the exhibitions is yet to be determined, but Newson's conversations with members of its future audience have made it clear that the museum will need to do more than simply entertain. "When we spoke to children about things that concern them, we discovered that there are a lot of serious things on their minds—the environment, famine, war, as well as things that happen in their daily life," he says. Including subjects like these in the museum's curation is a recognition that brute happiness is not the be-all and end-all of childhood. "You can't just be joyful the whole time—we also need to allow space for things that are difficult and challenging," says Newson.

In Western cultures, the dominant ideal for childhood is commonly understood to be one of cheerful innocence, play and learning. Individualistic cultures place particular emphasis on personal happiness as both an aspiration and an obligation—the United States Declaration of Independence explicitly guarantees its pursuit. But childhood is a mutable and culturally-embedded concept, not a concrete fact. In Europe, it was only around the Enlightenment that children began to be seen as worthy of protection from the hardships of adulthood; philosophers such as Jean-Jacques Rousseau started writing about

Having grown up straddling two cultures, Indian and British, our writer Debika says she saw first-hand that notions of "the good life" could be subjective. While happiness in an immediate sense was clearly a priority for her parents, so too was nurturing relationships with family, friends and community as the building blocks to future contentment.

education in a more child-centered way and advocating for a child's inherent good. In the Victorian era, although children were in practice still being sent down coal mines and up chimneys, a more sentimentalized view of children also emerged. Literature aimed specifically at entertaining rather than instructing became popular around this time, from Lewis Carroll's *Alice's Adventures in Wonderland* to Mark Twain's *Tom Sawyer*, and influential figures including Charles Darwin and Prince Albert in the UK became interested in child development.

KIDS' CORNER: This cloud looks full of rain. Turn to page 116 to learn about different cloud formations, and draw your own.

A focus on feelings became apparent only after World War II. "You can see the difference in parenting manuals when you look at those by Truby King in the 1930s, which talked about routines and training children out of crying, and the child-centered views of the likes of Benjamin Spock in 1946, who told mothers to trust themselves," says Heather Montgomery, Professor of Anthropology and Childhood at the Open University's Faculty of Wellbeing, Education and Language Studies.

Today, happiness is the main paradigm through which many cultures judge the "success" of a childhood, but what that means exactly is harder to say. A child is likely to choose play over study, but the latter may be the route to happiness in the long term. A parent may be tempted to shower their infant with gifts while being aware that this might make them less able to appreciate things later in life.

"You can't just be joyful the whole time — we also need to allow space for things that are difficult and challenging."

Liz Kleinrock, an educator who is part of our editorial board, says that in working with Black families and colleagues, the idea of which children are seen as deserving of an 'innocent' childhood comes up repeatedly. "For Black children who are often perceived as older and less 'innocent' than their same-aged white peers, this is something they often do not get to fully experience," Liz says.

The anthropologist David F. Lancy describes societies that value
children above all else (such as the US at present) as neontocracies,
while societies that primarily value older members are gerontocracies.
Lancy emphasizes that neontocracies are historically rare.

---

Happiness is also culturally relative. "Expressions of emotion differ so much across cultures that sometimes there aren't even common words to identify them," says Peggy Froerer, a reader in anthropology at Brunel University, who has researched childhood in several contexts.

Indeed, "happiness" is not a word that all parents choose when naming their parenting priorities. A recent survey found that 73% of Americans and 86% of people in France pointed to happiness as the most important goal in raising children, but only 49% of respondents in India did, compared with 51% who were more interested in success and achievement. Culture aside, the goal of pure happiness can often be a luxury for families facing other hardships. There's every reason to believe that almost all these parents want what is "best" for their children.

Maybe the word "happy" is too nebulous for something as high-stakes as the needs of children. Instead, many researchers, including Montgomery and her colleagues, are moving towards the term "wellbeing"—a relatively new addition to our emotional lexicon that's broad enough to encompass everything from security, to joy, to feeling valued.

Unlike happiness, wellbeing allows for the fact that so-called negative emotions are often appropriate—and recognizes that, while we continue to treat children differently from adults, they are also complex beings with various desires, needs and problems. "You wouldn't expect a child to be happy when experiencing crisis, bereavement, abuse or pain," says Amelia Roberts, deputy director at UCL's Centre for Inclusive Education, who is working on a project to support wellbeing and emotional resilience in schools. "Pop psychology pushes us towards a glib, positive thinking mantra, but when we tell a child not to cry or worry, we're often trying to move them quickly to a place that's more comfortable for us. It takes energy to understand someone's sadness or anger." One danger of this "toxic" happiness,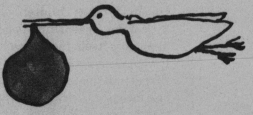

"Expressions of emotion differ so much across cultures that

she says, is that we aren't mindful of emotions that are trying to send us valuable signals. This seems more crucial than ever at a time when worries about children's mental health are on the rise in many countries. Nadim Saad, founder of consultancy the Happy Confident Company, also values emotional exploration in his work with children and parents. Despite his liberal use of the "H word", he makes clear that happiness is only one part of the equation. "It can only come after doing the hard work of understanding what's happening to us in difficult moments," he says. He echoes Roberts' sentiment about our discomfort with unpleasant feelings. "Children see their parents being anxious, but then they're told, 'don't worry' or 'don't cry'," he says. "What they hear is that what they're feeling isn't ok. It's important for children to develop their disappointment and their frustration muscles, so they know how to handle unpleasant feelings."

To "evolve the emotional vocabulary" of children, he encourages them to identify a long list of what they're feeling then narrow it down to a manageable number. "The eventual idea is to realize that feelings are triggered by thoughts," he says. "Then you can think about what you want to feel instead and how you can get there."

In dealing with what he says is a major source of unhappiness—the overwhelming number of choices available in today's complex world—he suggests encouraging children to make decisions from an early age, by regularly offering them a limited set of good options. "Asking them if they want to leave the house in five or 10 minutes gives children the impression of having power," he says. Of course, choices can sometimes wind up as mistakes. He advises that children get used to dealing with them by looking for learning opportunities. When it comes to happiness itself, his advice for children is similar to what it would be for adults. "I ask children to write down three things that made it a good day—whether it's the weather or a nice meal," he says. "Happiness is often about appreciating the small things in life."

A final trouble with the term happiness, or at least the way we use it, is that its connotations are heavily

sometimes there aren't common words to identify them."

individualistic—entangled in the language of personal fulfillment, actualization, self-care and acquisition. But of course, our emotional state cannot be separated from our social context. "That's why developing empathy and compassion, by telling children to put themselves in other people's shoes, is important," says Saad, adding that acts of kindness are proven to make you happier.

Actions, after all—tangible, deliberate and mindful— are the physical manifestations of how we feel. That's why, at the Museum of Childhood, nurturing creativity and creative expression is such a central focus. "For children, creating something beautiful or useful is really important," Newson says. "As a parent, I know that when my daughter has agency over making something, the joy it gives her is incredibly powerful." **k**

KIDS' CORNER: How many happy faces can you find in the magazine?

Living in Delhi in the 1990s, our writer Debika remembers a children's newspaper called *News Joy* as one of her primary sources of happiness and inspiration. The paper, which published games, jokes and birthday shout outs (with very little news) spawned a cottage industry of DIY newspapers in her household.

# EMOTIONS
# Name that face!

Helping your child to develop an emotional vocabulary gives them an important tool to use for self-expression and when asking for help. Even at a young age, children can learn the nuances of emotions, such as the difference between "disappointed" and "frustrated." When your child says they feel "bad" or "good," can you prompt them to be more specific in explaining how they feel? Try reading picture books together and asking your child how the characters might feel throughout the story; encourage them to use visual cues (such as facial expressions) or make personal connections by asking them to recall times when they felt a similar emotion.

The six faces on this page are all expressing common emotions. Ask your child to identify the emotions pictured. If their answers differ slightly from the ones written, that's okay. Ask your child how they got to each answer. What clues did they pick up on in the face? What did it remind them of?

EXCITED
HAPPY
FRUSTRATED
SURPRISED
DISAPPOINTED
SAD

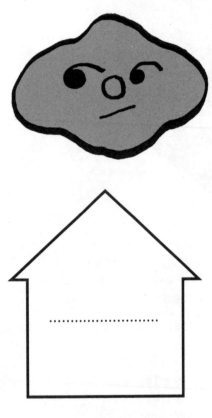

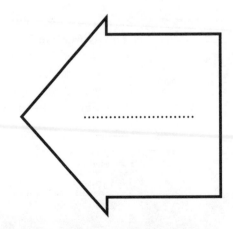

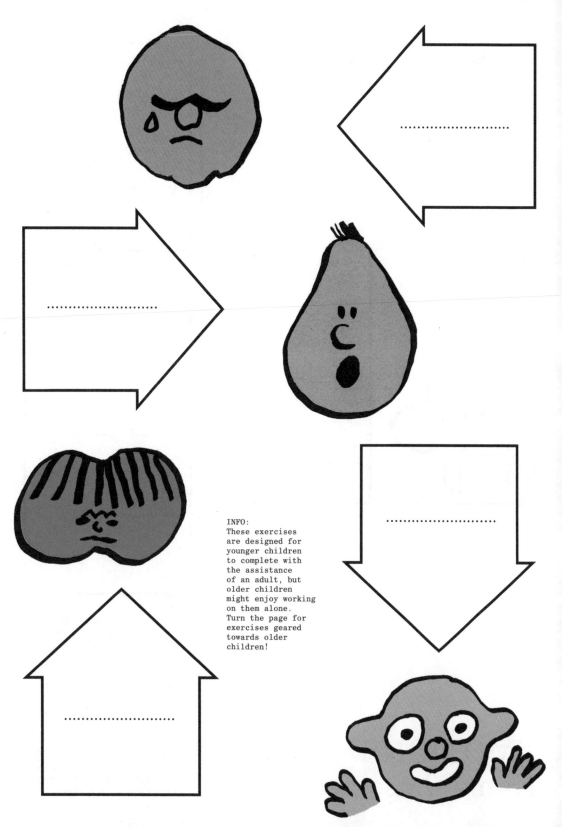

INFO:
These exercises
are designed for
younger children
to complete with
the assistance
of an adult, but
older children
might enjoy working
on them alone.
Turn the page for
exercises geared
towards older
children!

| Question: | Answer: | Question: |
|---|---|---|
| WHEN I FEEL NERVOUS, WHAT MAKES ME FEEL CALM? | ............................. ............................. ............................. ............................. ............................. ............................. ............................. ............................. ............................. | WHEN I FEEL FRUSTRATED, HOW CAN I USE MY WORDS TO ASK OTHERS FOR WHAT I NEED? |

**Answer:**

.............................

.............................

.............................

.............................

.............................

.............................

.............................

# EMOTIONS
## Name those needs!

These questions are designed to help your children proactively think about how they can respond to their emotions once they've identified them. These can be particularly helpful tools for developing independence by learning how to share and balance emotions in situations when there may not be an adult present to assist. There's space to write answers on this page, or you can use the questions as prompts for conversations.

**Question:**

WHEN I FEEL EXCITED, HOW CAN I SHARE MY FEELINGS WITH MY FRIENDS AND FAMILY?

**Answer:**

..............................

..............................

..............................

..............................

..............................

..............................

..............................

..............................

**Question:**

WHEN I FEEL IMPATIENT, HOW CAN I REMIND MYSELF TO SLOW DOWN?

**Answer:**

..............................

..............................

..............................

..............................

..............................

**NOW TRY THIS:**

Kids GROK is a wonderful card game and tool designed by Jean Morrison and Christine King, both certified trainers through the Center for Nonviolent Communication (CNVC). The premise of Nonviolent Communication is that everything everyone says or does is to meet a need or value, and this game supports children in identifying their feelings and needs in a variety of ways.

**Question:**

WHEN I FEEL LOVED, HOW CAN I SHOW PEOPLE WHO LOVE ME HOW MUCH I APPRECIATE THEM?

**Answer:**

..............................

..............................

..............................

..............................

..............................

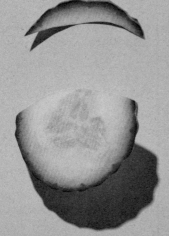

# EAT YOUR
## WORDS:

COOL AS A CUCUMBER:
This expression was
first recorded in
a 1732 poem about
unrequited love by
John Gay: "Pert
as a pear-monger
I'd be / If Molly
were but kind; /
Cool as a cucumber
could see / The
rest of womankind."
The meaning was
probably literal:
because cucumbers
have such high
water content,
they are often
appreciably cooler
than the external
atmosphere.

DON'T GIVE A FIG:
The mild-mann-
ered cousin of
a far fruitier
expression, "to
not give a fig"
dates back to
Shakespearean
times. It evolved
from a Spanish hand
gesture—placing the
thumb between the
first and second
fingers to signal
contempt—that came
to be known as The
Fig of Spain.

Fruity feelings find
        a fresh, fun form.

FULL OF BEANS:
In 14th-century
Europe, stable
masters would feed
horses a diet
of beans grown
specifically for
fodder. After
noticing how much
energy the animals
had after eating,
the phrase "full of
beans" was used to
describe bursts of
liveliness—and has
been ever since.

RED AS A BEET:
In the Victorian
era, when wearing
a full face of
makeup was frowned
upon, women would
discretely apply
the juice of beets
to their cheeks
to give a rosier
complexion—a
"blush" that gave
way to describing
cheeks flushed from
embarrassment today.

TOUGH NUT TO CRACK:
The origin of this
straightforward
metaphor is a tough
nut to crack, but
it was used by
Benjamin Franklin
as far back as
1754. In a letter
to his brother
describing US
efforts to capture
a French Canadian
fortress, he wrote:
"...fortified towns
are hard nuts to
crack; and your
teeth have not been
accustomed to it."

PEACHY-KEEN:
A mid-century
Americanism meaning
"everything's just
fine." The first
written reference
appeared in *Time*
magazine in a
1948 profile of
gregarious Pasadena
disc jockey
Jim Hawthorne;
some believe it
was Hawthorne
that coined the
phrase. The writer
also described
Hawthorne's lingo
as "banana-split."

Psychology professor.
Pixar consultant. Parent.

knows what's going on
inside your child's head.

For the past three decades, Dacher Keltner has made a study of human emotions. As a psychology professor at the University of California at Berkeley and author of such books as *The Compassionate Instinct* and *Born to Be Good*, Keltner has examined how emotions like sympathy and joy have shaped our evolutionary development as sentient beings—and why all of us are, at our core, nicer than the cynics would have us believe. If you've seen the 2015 Pixar movie *Inside Out*, for which Keltner served as a consultant, you might think there are five emotions, from exuberant, blue-haired Joy, to curmudgeonly red-faced Anger, with jets of flame where his hairline should be. But there are actually 20, says Keltner, and they all sort of get along. "There's a Western European view of the mind at war, but I don't think that aligns with what the emotions are like," he says. "They actually help us do good things in the world."

These days, when Keltner isn't teaching classes or writing books, he serves as faculty director of Berkeley's Greater Good Science Center and hosts the podcast *The Science of Happiness*, which he launched in 2018. The professor and father spoke to *Kindling* about why some kids are happier than others, why toddlers are kinder than you think, and what a parent can do to raise more emotionally open children—regardless of their own upbringing.

"One way to think about emotions
              is that they're like characters."

RI:     People often think that there are good emotions, like joy, and bad ones, like anger. Is that correct?

DK:     One of the oldest ideas held by a lot of people, less so in East Asian traditions but very much so in Judeo-Christian traditions, is that emotions are disruptive. In actuality, all of the emotions have a point, right? They've been built into us by evolution. One of my favorite examples is anger, which can lead you to do really inappropriate things, but can also lead you to protest things that are unfair.

RI:     In *Inside Out*, we see the emotions chit-chat and bicker and work together within Riley's brain. Did the filmmakers do a good job of capturing the inner life of an 11-year-old girl?

DK: I was blown away. One of my favorite examples is how emotion influences our memories. Part of the movie is about how Riley remembers her past in Minnesota, and how emotions like sadness can change how we remember things. There's actually a researcher named Linda Levine who's done this amazing work showing how the way we feel right now leads us to reconstruct our past. So if I'm feeling happy and content, I'll look back on my high school years and feel like they were okay. They showed that in *Inside Out* with the core "memory orbs", which turn blue when Sadness touches them.

RI: In the movie, the five emotions are imagined as people. Is it helpful, as a scientist, to think of them as such?

DK: I think so. Emotions are these really complicated, subjective experiences, so how do you explain what they are? I think one way that we think about emotions is that they have character, or they're like a character. There are people who have analyzed the world's literature in terms of different emotions—that there are sad stories, stories of courage or righteousness and shame and so forth. So when we talk about emotions, characters are not a bad way to think about it.

KIDS' CORNER: If sadness was a character, what would it look like? Draw a picture!

RI: What do parents misunderstand about childhood emotions?

DK: I think we misunderstand a lot. One thing we should know is that it's okay to be sad, and that being sad is different to depression. When young kids hit 13 or 14, especially girls, they get a little bit more anxious and sad, but that's just a developmental occurrence as they hit puberty. And then we panic, and we medicate it. But they're gonna change out of that.

I also think we misunderstand the urge to play and to be silly. Kids really need to be silly. It's so good for them. Laughing is good, play is essential. Sometimes we look at laughter and we feel like, *oh, those kids aren't being serious, what they're doing isn't important.* But it's some of the most important stuff they do.

RI:     Are some kids just born happier or sadder?

DK:     Yes. Part of the American myth is that you can become as happy as you want, but the raw fact is that about half of our emotional lives on a daily basis is genetically inherited. You get this complex pattern of genes in your body, and it influences neurotransmitters and that shapes your emotion. And it means some kids are just easier, and some are gonna have a lot more anxiety, like I did. And that's okay, you know? You can change. But temperament is a big thing in our life.

RI:     You've written a lot about the importance of compassion. How early on do we see compassion in children?

DK:     We used to think of compassion as this act of culture, as something learned, but now we know it's just part of who we are. It's a human universal. There's a fellow named Michael Tomasello who's doing these great studies showing that for kids at 18 months, seeing other people suffer really registers. They'll do things to help an adult, they'll put a Band-Aid on someone, they'll take care of someone who's crying.

"Some kids are just easier, and some
        are gonna have a lot more anxiety, like I did.
And that's okay, you know? You can change."

Dacher was photographed in his garden in BERKELEY, CALIFORNIA.

Pixar often
consults
experts like
Dacher. For
*Soul* (2020),
the team spoke
to religious
leaders for
a variety of
perspectives on
the nature of
the soul.

RI:     You've also talked about the importance of touch in communicating compassion.

DK:     It's interesting, I started to do work on touch and compassion right about when I had my daughters, and I realized the amount of deep connection that comes through playing with them and carrying them, soothing them and hugging them, singing lullabies and rubbing their heads at night. There's new work coming out of Israel showing that those early interactions with your young kids, those first five years of being close to them, when they hear your voice and your hand is on their back, that that is the foundation of compassion: I'm connected to another human being, I feel the same as them.

RI:     Growing up, I was always taught that you shouldn't cry. Was that bad advice?

DK:     Yeah. That was very bad advice.

RI:     Let's say you're not the most emotive parent, and when I say you, I mean me. Can you still raise emotionally healthy kids?

DK:     Totally! Number one is: do you allow your kids to be aware of their emotions, as opposed to just shutting them down? So instead of saying, "Stop crying," you say, "You seem sad, why is that?" So you allow for that. Teaching children a vocabulary is fundamental, too. You don't have to be the most emotional person, but if you're saying to a child things like "How are you feeling?" "Does that make you angry or sad?" "Is that embarrassing to you?" then you're giving them this vocabulary. That's really important. **k**

105 — 120

And now for the fun stuff! All games and activities designed by Emma Scott-Child.

CAN YOU SPOT A CUT-OUT CLAUDE?

# Fun Stuff

# A WELL-TRODDEN WALK

## Four ways to make a regular route feel like a brand-new adventure.

Task 01:

### PAVEMENT BINGO

Write a list of things that you might find along a route you always walk (or a few you might not), take it with you and tick them off as you go. Rather than listing objects, you could think about different groups of things: for example, things that are yellow, or that start with the letter "B". On another day, you could look for things that make you feel happy, afraid or calm.

### MAKE AN ART INSTALLATION

Choose something that you might find along the way and collect a group of them, like leaves, twigs or stones. When you get home, arrange them into a circle or a pattern like an Andy Goldsworthy* installation. You could arrange leaves and petals into a rainbow spectrum, sort pebbles from small to large, or create a spiral out of sticks.

*

## WHOSE CAR IS THAT?

Imagine that certain color cars belong to different characters from your favorite books and films. Have a think about who would drive a green car—maybe Shrek? Call out the characters' names as you see their cars. Choose unusual colors to keep it fun.

## GOOD TO KNOW

—

* You might find that toddlers love to line up similar objects. This is their way of figuring out how things fit together. They are making sense of the similarities and differences in size, shape, color and texture. Sorting is a great activity for their cognitive development. Have a look at the work of artist Andy Goldsworthy to see this taken to a beautiful extreme.

"YOU COULD HOP, SHAKE YOUR LEGS ABOUT, JUMP AROUND IN A CIRCLE, OR FLAP YOUR ARMS LIKE A CHICKEN."

## MINISTRY OF SILLY WALKS

Pretend you're in Monty Python's *Ministry of Silly Walks*. Make up a really funny way of walking. You could hop, shake your legs about, jump around in a circle, or flap your arms like a chicken. It's up to you! The other person has to copy you. Do they dare to walk down the road being this silly?

| Task 02: | FACE TIME |
| --- | --- |
| * | The house is full of faces, if you know where to find them. |

GRUMPY FACE:
Staffan and Linn
used a book for a
face, an egg and
washer for eyes,
a pencil for a
mustache, a potato
masher for a mouth
and a deer antler
for a nose—Linn
found one in her
garden in Finland!

# INSTRUCTIONS:

The way we move our faces can tell people how we're feeling inside. Sometimes we do it without even knowing. How often have you looked at someone you like, then realized you're giving them a big smile? Or maybe you've felt unsure about something and then realized that you're scrunching your eyebrows and making a furrowed brow. Let's have a think about how our faces can tell others about our emotions. First, we'll need some blank faces—you could use plates, chopping boards, paper or pans. Anything flat will work. Now gather objects around your house that will become our facial features: eyes, eyebrows, nose and mouth. You could try using coins, pasta, pencils, pebbles, bottle tops, shoelaces, scissors and spoons. If you want to add hair, you could use socks, string or scrunched-up tissue paper. Arrange the objects on each surface to make a face.

TRY TO MAKE THESE EMOTIONS:
Surprised
Grumpy
Excited
Nervous
Proud
Angry

Remember to put it all back where you found it when you're done!

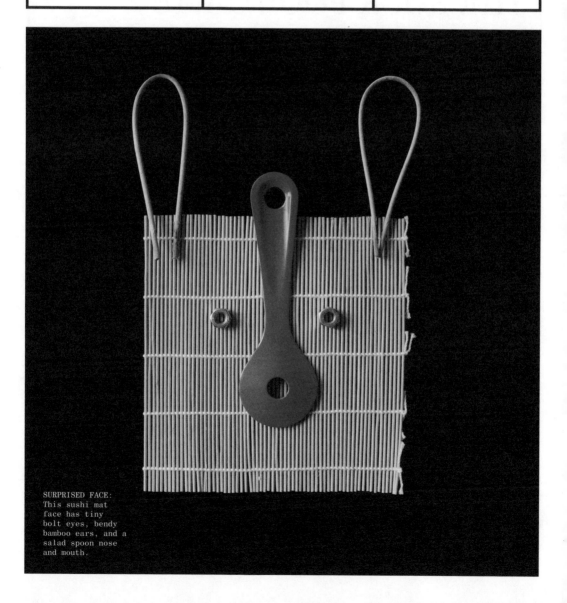

SURPRISED FACE:
This sushi mat face has tiny bolt eyes, bendy bamboo ears, and a salad spoon nose and mouth.

# THE ROCK POOL GAME

## Make crafty cutouts and play spot the difference.

### Task 03:

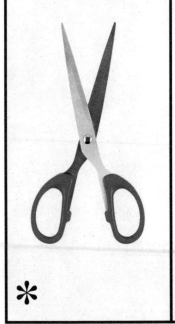

*

First, we're going to craft some simple rock pools full of colorful fish and shells, and then we'll use them to play different games. To make the rock pools, you'll need bright paper: You could also use colored felt, card, or paper that you've painted yourself. Draw some shapes onto the paper that look like things you might find in a rock pool. Keep the shapes bold and simple in different colors. You might have a starfish, some seaweed, some coral, fish and shells.

Cut them out and then trace around each one to create another set of the same shapes. Cut these out too so you end up with two sets of identical shapes. You'll also need two identical backgrounds, ideally blue or green. Now that you have all your pieces, you can play some games with them.

**MATCHING ROCK POOLS**
One person creates a picture with one set of shapes, arranging the objects in their rock pool. The other has to recreate the exact same picture using the second set of shapes. To make it extra tricky, show the picture for only 10 seconds and then cover it up.

**SPOT THE DIFFERENCE**
One person makes two rock pool pictures that are almost identical, and the other has to spot the differences.

**DOUBLE UP**
For this game, lay one set of shapes out on the background and double up on just one shape from the other set. How quickly can the other person spot the double?

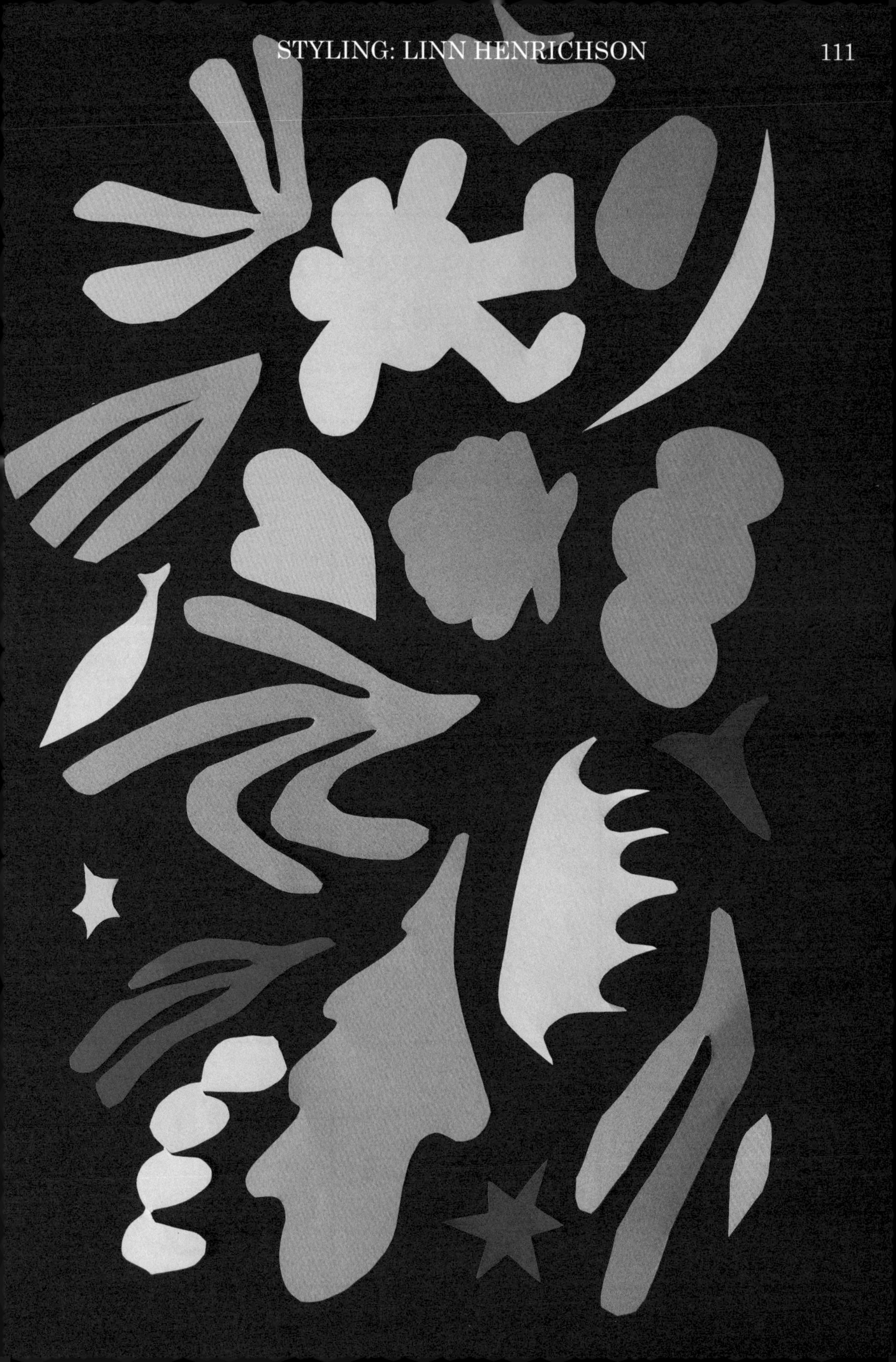

# DARWIN'S BIRDS

## What adaptations would help the birds in your neighborhood?

Nearly 200 years ago, Charles Darwin studied finches on the Galapagos Islands and discovered that the same species of bird appeared on several islands but that each had adapted differently to their surroundings. The finches didn't leave their islands and had no natural predators, so they bred easily. Over many generations, their bodies changed and grew into different shapes according to their different needs. Darwin found that finches with narrow beaks ate small insects, while finches that cracked through hard nuts and seeds to get their food had bigger, stronger beaks. Darwin made a scientific log of his findings and recorded the details of each bird. This research formed the basis of his theories of natural selection and evolution.

## Task 04:

*

Imagine if the birds in your neighborhood had adapted to the surroundings in which you live. What would they look like? What sort of funny features might they have?

Think of some different places in your neighborhood, then imagine that some magnificently weird birds have adapted to these places. Imagine an ice-cream shop finch. It might be covered in spots that look like sprinkles with a cherry-shaped feather on its head to blend into its surroundings, or a fire station finch that has grown feathery earmuffs to block out the sound of sirens. Maybe a bird that lives in a fountain would grow an umbrella on its head to keep dry.

Draw a picture of
your wonderful
local creature,
just like Charles
Darwin did.

Name:

.................................

Place found:

.................................

Features:

.................................

Eats:

.................................

Sounds like:

.................................

DRAW A PICTURE:

# DUCKS IN A ROW

The *Kindling* ducks look to the sky for meaning.

Sarah says this comic was inspired by how she and her sisters used to squabble about what they could see in the clouds. "As an adult, all that I see now is the doom and gloom of the gray skies!" She is still holding out to one day see a crocodile-shaped cloud.

# Seriously fun science & art projects

Hands-on learning for kids of all ages!

Arcade
from Kiwi Crate

Birds
from Koala Crate

Get **50% off** your first month!

Visit **kiwico.com/kindling**

# CLOUD WATCH

## Learn the names of common clouds, then draw your own!

CIRRUS

CUMULUS

CUMULONIMBUS

.............................

maileg

A storymaking company...

www.maileg.com

# bitte

SUSTAINABLE CLASSICS FOR MODERN KIDS

ARKET
arket.com

BABAÀ
babaa.es

BEX SPORT
bexsport.com

BIRKENSTOCK
birkenstock.com

BONPOINT
bonpoint.com

CO LABEL
colabel.dk

DR. MARTENS
drmartens.com

FIN AND VINCE
finandvince.com

FJÄLLRÄVEN
fjallraven.com

HAY
hay.com

INDUSTRY OF ALL NATIONS
industryofallnations.com

JENNIFER FISHER
jenniferfisherjewelry.com

JENNY BIRD
jenny-bird.com

MABO
mabokids.com

MISHA AND PUFF
misha-and-puff.com

MOLO
molo.com

NANUSHKA
nanushka.com

NOBLE CARRIAGE
noblecarriage.com

OEUF
oeufnyc.com

OLLIELLA
olliella.com

PARACHUTE BROOKLYN
parachutebrooklyn.com

PRADA
prada.com

TEKLA
tekla.com

THE FRANKIE SHOP
thefrankieshop.com

ZARA
zara.com

P. 26, 27, 79, 106, 107, 110, 112 & 113
Images: Shutterstock

P. 22
ABILITY
*Gender Bias in Mothers' Expectations about Infant Crawling*, Journal of Experimental Child Psychology, 2000

PRAISE
*Parent Praise to 1-3 Year-Olds Predicts Children's Motivational Frameworks 5 Years Later*, Child Development, 2013

RISK
*Mothers' Responses to Boys and Girls Engaging in Injury-Risk Behaviors on a Playground*, The Journal of Experimental Child Psychology, 2000

PAIN
*Gender Bias in Pediatric Pain Assessment*, Journal of Pediatric Psychology, 2019

*Gender Stereotypes about Intellectual Ability Emerge Early and Influence Children's Interests*, Science, 2017

*Gender in Children's Television Worldwide*, Televizion, 2008

SPECIAL THANKS
Elaine Burns
Katie Gauld
Linn Henrichson
The two *Kindling* babies, coming 2021 courtesy of Alex and Jess. We can't wait to meet you both!

# OPEN HERE IN CASE OF EMERGENCY

## Five super simple ways to have fun *right* now.

### 1. READY, STEADY, DRAW!

This is a game where we draw things quickly and see how funny they can be. Write down random things, objects and animals on small pieces of paper and then put them in a pot. Take out two pieces of paper at a time, set a timer for two minutes and draw those two things together. You might end up with a monkey on a cactus, or a carrot wearing socks.

### 2. HONEY AND GRAVEL

Twist your brain into some abstract thinking. Taking it in turns, one person says a word and the other has to think of what the opposite might be. The opposite of something small would be big, or the opposite of something fluffy might be hard. There are no right or wrong answers, you've just got to have a good reason for your suggestion. For example, the opposite of honey might be gravel because one is rough and the other one smooth.

### 3. THE WISHING WELL

Make a circle out of masking tape or rope on the floor and throw coins into it like it's a wishing well. As you throw each coin in, make a silly wish about the person you're playing the game with, like "I wish you were a cat!" If you get it in the circle, your wish comes true and the other person has to pretend to be a cat. The older you are, the smaller the circle gets!

### 4. THE DISGUST-ING PIZZA GAME

Imagine you're ordering a pizza. Each person takes a turn to add a disgusting topping to the pizza, but you have to remember the ones before. So, you might say: "I ordered a pizza and I asked for one with zebra poop." The next person says, "I ordered a pizza and I asked for one with zebra poop and troll snot..." See how many toppings you can remember in a row.

### 5. FACE SCULPTURES

Take some Scotch tape and tape your face into a funny position. Make a pig nose, tape your mouth into a new position or stick your eyebrows up to look surprised. See how silly you can make yourself look. Try not to get the tape on your hair.